Death Of The Dollar

The Prepper's DIY Guide To Bartering, Surviving An Economic Collapse And The Death Of Money

By Henry Hill

Contents

Introduction

Chapter 1
What Could Possibly Cause a Financial Collapse?

Chapter 2
What To Expect If Money Becomes Worthless

Chapter 3
How To Survive In A World Where Money Is Of Little Value
The Skills You Need To Learn
Strengthening Your Position
What You Need To Stockpile

Chapter 4
Cashless Economics 101

Conclusion

"Paper is poverty,... it is only the ghost of money, and not money itself." --Thomas Jefferson 1788

Introduction

Preppers are often scoffed at for their belief in preparing for doomsday or something equally disastrous. They have received a bad reputation as people who are waiting for the sky to fall and hoarding food and guns while running around wearing camo and hiding in the trees. Unfortunately, that is a false misconception that has been cultivated by those who are not familiar with preppers and what they do.

The reasons preppers stockpile food and water vary, but all can agree that the state of the economy is reason to be concerned and is one of the leading reasons people choose to start building up emergency supplies of food, water, and basic necessities. There is a real risk of the economy completely dropping out. An economic collapse would ultimately be more devastating than a natural disaster that just affected one part of the country. An economic collapse would have a chain reaction throughout the entire world. It would affect trade deals, which would cause economic strife in the countries that relied upon the business of the country that failed.

Fortunately, we haven't had to deal with a major economic crisis in nearly a hundred years, but there are signs we are headed in that direction. We barely avoided a calamity in 2008, but it was by the very skin of our teeth.

What will you do if the economy fails? A true collapse would result in the downward spiral of the world as we know it. Could you feed your family after a failure? Could you keep them safe from thieves who want to take what you have? If you are not prepared, then no you couldn't.

In today's world, you go to work to earn wages to pay for the things you want and need. Your job relies on the doors being open for business. Businesses rely on the ability to sell a product or service to paying customers. When there is no money to pay employees, there will be no product or service to offer. You won't have a job. Your normal routine, consisting of getting up and taking a hot shower before heading off to work, stops. Coming home and watching television while eating dinner is no longer an option. Now, you are forced to rely on what you have in your pantry today for food or rely on your skills to hunt and fish.

You can do something to prepare for that situation. Only the prepared will survive such a major catastrophe. This book will help you do what is necessary to survive an economic downturn. Start today to prepare your family to survive in a world where paper money means nothing and commerce is non-existent. A world where all the stocks and bonds you invested in are worth nothing.

Chapter 1

What Could Possibly Cause A Financial Collapse?

Before you quickly dismiss the idea that a financial collapse will ever happen, you need to read the following list. There are some very real scenarios that can lead to a total financial crisis that would affect economies all around the world. You don't have to buy into all of these scenarios, but you should consider them carefully. Sticking your head in the sand and pretending everything is fine and dandy is dangerous. Any one of these events can happen. We have seen it before. Our economy today is barely getting by. We are hanging on by our fingertips. If the economy was a little healthier, one of these events could be tolerated. Unfortunately, we have already suffered one or all of these over the past couple of decades and we are walking on shaky ground.

There have been plenty of near misses over the past decade. We have managed to skate by, but each close call has left consumers a little wary. Wary consumers make for a difficult economy that will struggle to recover.

Major Market Crash

Stock markets are finicky. Recently, we witnessed a small downturn in the wake of the Ebola crisis in 2014. When Ebola started crossing borders, the public panicked and the stock market reflected those concerns. When people are scared, they quickly lose faith in the

People trying to withdraw their money from the bank during the market crash of 1929

financial system. Any time there is a disaster or crisis people get shaken up and tighten the purse strings. They don't want to spend their money in case they lose their jobs tomorrow. Investors decide to cut and run and the stock market plummets. Politics also play a role in the stock market. If people don't like the president or other world leaders, it will affect the way they spend. Normally, it rebounds fairly quickly, but imagine if something major happened—another war, a major pandemic or a severe natural disaster. It could take several months or years for the economy to recover. Jobs would be lost, homes would be foreclosed, and businesses would be shuttered.

Hyperinflation

There have been plenty of dire predictions from expert economists about hyperinflation. It is predicted to happen within the next 10 years. We have seen some signs of this already happening. Technically, low to moderate

A one hundred trillion note from Zimbabwe's period of inflation of 2006

inflation indicates the economy is healthy. When prices rise a little on the things we need and want, it is a good thing—according to the experts. However, hyperinflation is when the cost of goods rises by let's say 50 percent. For example, that gallon of milk for which you currently pay $3.00 would jump to $150 over a period of months. Nobody could afford to pay for the milk or anything else. The subject of hyperinflation happening in the United States is one that divides the experts. Some are convinced it couldn't happen, while others insist we are headed in that direction. A quick look at the history of other major economies like China, Germany, and Russia all prove that it most certainly can happen and has happened in the past.

Deflation

On the flip side of hyperinflation, we run the risk of deflation. Back in 2010, we saw the first signs of deflation when the price of oil dropped. Now, in 2014, we are seeing oil prices drop down to what they were back then. That has some economists a little worried. While we are thrilled to be able to afford to drive our cars again, investors and economists start ringing the doomsday bell. People start pinching pennies because the experts are telling us an economic crash is imminent. That means the economy starts to tank with consumers holding onto their money instead of spending it and feeding the profits of businesses around the world. That means folks are going to be losing their jobs because businesses are struggling. It is similar to a snowball rolling downhill. Deflation can be blamed for extending the Great Depression for years. Deflation is dangerous because consumers know if they hold out just a few more weeks or months, that item they have had their eye on is going to drop in price. On the surface, deflation appears to be a positive thing for consumers. Unfortunately, deflation is a slow way down to the bottom.

Natural Disaster

A natural disaster that affects large cities, like New York or Los Angeles, or destroys oil rigs can cause major financial upheaval. A disaster that interrupts the flow of goods from one city to the next can have long last repercussions. The prediction of a disaster striking will affect the stock market. We saw this with Hurricane Sandy. Traders were concerned about the fate of a major metropolis and got antsy. If a natural disaster were to cause major damage and interrupt the supply chain, prices on certain goods would skyrocket. The increase in prices would make it impossible for people to buy the things they needed. People would have to do without the item or cut out other expenses to get what they absolutely needed. No matter the scenario, it would result in a slow, but steady economic collapse. The duration of the collapse would depend on the severity of the disaster and how long it took the area to recover.

War

War, big or small, could devastate an economy. Not only is war incredibly expensive, it destroys citizens' trust in their leaders. They are terrified to spend money and in many cases, can't spend the money because the war has destroyed various businesses and reduced supply. People can't go to work like they normally would. That means less output of goods the rest of the world has come to rely on. Demand will be high, which will result in skyrocketing prices. War and economic failure will result in civil unrest. It is a recipe for a major financial crisis that may take years or decades to recover from. War will leave people living with very little tangible possessions and unwilling to buy more just in case they are destroyed by war. War leaves people uneasy and more apt to hunker down at home unwilling to spend money—if they have any.

Citizens Unhappy with Government

Citizens in every nation will also be a little irritated with their government. Nobody can please everybody one hundred percent of the time. However, more and more citizens in various countries are fighting back. They are tired of the way governments are operating. This leads to civil unrest and unwillingness to buy into things like stocks, bonds, and other ways to feed the government. All it takes is a single act or a new law or tax to spur civil unrest. When millions of people get together and riot, the economic toll would spawn a major financial collapse. The most recent example of civil unrest caused mainly by economic hardship is in Belgium. With the financial crisis getting worse instead of better, cutbacks will be made, which will further drive citizens into debt and poverty. Riots in Ferguson, Missouri were spawned by an officer involved shooting. A single incident can lead to widespread discontent that destroys businesses and causes major damage which results in damages costing millions of dollars to repair.

Chapter 2

What To Expect If Money Becomes Worthless

If the economy collapses and the dollar becomes worthless, what will happen? We have heard about the value of the dollar, the euro, and the yen dropping for years. Money becomes worthless if the government issuing the currency doesn't have the funds to back it or is basically broke. There are plenty of countries in the world right now that are in serious debt. The debt decreases the value of the currency. If the debt continues to increase and there is no hope of ever getting out of that debt, the currency will eventually become worthless.

If that happens, the thousands of dollars you have in your bank account will be worth nothing more than a few pennies in today's world. It is a little hard to imagine a world without paper money.
The following are a few things you can expect to happen if money becomes worthless.

- Without money, there will be no way to pay for goods and services. That means you can't run to the store to buy food or go to the hospital for medical help because doctors don't work for free. Hospitals will close their doors with no funding.

- Banks will fail. The home you live in, if you have a mortgage, isn't yours. It isn't even the bank's. It belongs to the person who bought the loan. It is estimated there are at least six claims on any single loan. The bank loaned you the money, but somebody loaned the bank the money, and that came from somebody else. There are a lot of hands in a single pot of cash.

- You won't be able to use your worthless money to try and buy things off your neighbours. Paper money could possibly be used for toilet paper or tinder bundle material, but that is about it.

- If the dollar fails, it will have a ripple effect that will result in the collapsing of economies all around the world. Imported goods will no longer trickle into the United States, which will put workers all around the world out of jobs.

- Transportation will cease without the ability to refuel.

- The power grid will fail; our world will go dark.

- Sanitation systems will grind to a halt. Clean drinking water will not be available. You won't be able to flush your toilets.

- Civil unrest, violence, and gangs will make life dangerous. With no paid law enforcement, unruliness will spread.

- Communication systems will fail. Your cell phone will stop working within a few weeks. Ham radios and listening to AM stations will be your only means of communicating with the outside world.

Basically, life as you know it will cease to exist. We simply cannot function on paper money forever. Compare it to watching a speeding train heading towards the end of an unfinished track. It's headed that way. We are waiting and watching. Will you prepare for the fallout or stare in horror at the disaster?

Once it becomes obvious that the fall is imminent, there is going to be a mad rush on stores to buy as much as possible before the banks shutter and the money we once relied upon becomes worthless. There will be a panic as people realize the future is uncertain and life as they know it is over. Those who didn't take the time to prepare or heed the warnings are going to be scrambling.

The following list includes some of the things that will be the first to disappear when the news spreads that the world's financial system is tanking.

- Generators
- Solar panels
- Fuel—all types, including small propane tanks used for cook stoves
- Guns, ammunition, and other weapons like tasers and pepper spray
- Water purification methods
- Baby items i.e. diapers, wipes, formula
- Medicine and first aid supplies
- Food
- Manual kitchen tools i.e. can openers, grain grinders
- Portable toilets, camp showers
- Feminine hygiene products
- Personal hygiene items i.e. soap, toilet paper
- Survival gear hunting knives, tents, camp stoves
- Flashlights, batteries, candles, matches, lighters
- Duct tape

- Seeds

Eventually, stores will be wiped out of everything. Looters will be in full force. Looters will take things simply because they can and hope to profit on the booty they steal down the road. Anybody who wasn't prepared will be forced to do without some basic necessities. Don't wait until the last minute! Get what you need today!

The Historical Precedents And The Current State Of Affairs

It is inevitable the dollar will fall. Throughout history, there have been hundreds of currencies that have collapsed. This may happen due to the dissolving of a government or because in an attempt to save a fledgling economy, the government created hyperinflation. With the way the economy is headed, that may be the only option left. Despite what we have been told, the economy is not getting any better. We have been fortunate enough to have made it this far on our paper money. The bottom is due to fall out.

The value of the American dollar has declined by 95 percent over the past 50 years. There isn't much farther for it to drop. Those who are saving up thousands of dollars in cash under the mattresses or even in the bank are going to be sitting on giant wads of worthless paper.

Recently, we got a taste of what financial collapse would look like. In 2010, just a little over a year after the crash of the stock market in 2008, banks failed. Because all banks are connected in one way or another, we watched numerous big businesses crumble. Insurance giant, AIG, was broke after one company went bankrupt. All money in the world is linked. When one major bank fails, it sets off a chain reaction. The housing bubble exploded, leaving banks holding the bag with nothing to back up their losses. The worldwide economy has yet to recover from that devastating hit.

Blame has been thrown around, but the real problem was choosing to believe the system was infallible. Regulators got lazy and banks got inflated egos and assumed they could write a check with funds they didn't have with the hope the money would somehow magically appear before the check cleared.

Another example is Detroit, Michigan. The city is known for its auto industry, but after the crash in 2008, it has struggled to recover. With major automakers closing their doors, the city fell apart. The decline didn't happen overnight. It took 40 years of poor money management and over-borrowing to finally catch up to the city.

Image above shows the current state of many parts of Detroit due to the economic trouble the once prosperous city is currently in.

Detroit is an example of what happens when financial crisis hits. Crime rates in the failing city have skyrocketed and there is no money to pay police to stop it. Imagine if the entire nation were to fall into bankruptcy like Detroit. The city has topped the country in the number of violent crimes for five years running. There are more murders in Detroit than there are days in the year. What is even scarier is the fact that even though the population of the city is steadily declining, the number of violent crimes continues to increase. This can all be blamed on the economic hardship of those stuck living in the city. It wreaks havoc on society.

Chapter 3

How To Survive In A World Where Money Is Of Little Value

When the economy tanks, life doesn't stop. The resourceful and prepared will survive—even thrive. Think back to a few hundred years ago, before paper money was first brought into the market place. Our ancestors relied on gold and silver. Paper money was built on the back gold and silver. You have to admit, it is a heck of a lot easier to carry around a few hundred dollars in paper money than it would be to carry around a bag of heavy gold.

While the prospect of losing thousands of dollars is scary, it isn't the end of the world. There are things you can do to make your life fairly comfortable and eventually you will learn a new normal without paper money. You have to change the way you think and do things.

You will have to learn to depend on yourself and learn to protect what is yours. You won't be able to call 911 to help you stop the robbers in your home. If you cannot adequately defend your property, it will be taken from you. There is a strong possibility gangs of bandits will eventually run you out of your home. They will take what they want by force.

Ownership of a home or building is going to be a non-issue considering the loan you used to buy the house has fallen through. What you claim as yours, will be refuted.

The Skills You Need To Learn

Without paper money, you are going to have to rely on yourself. You can't buy bread—you have to make it. You can't run the washing machine—you are going to have to wash by hand. You won't be able to buy fruits and veggies—you have to grow everything.

In today's world, we have become lazy. We don't have to rely on our hands to do much of anything except open the refrigerator or push the buttons on a microwave. It is time to relearn the ways of our ancestors. Learning how to be self-sufficient is a skill that will benefit you no matter if the financial collapse occurs in your lifetime or not. You can save money by learning to be more self-reliant. Learning how to set up a solar power energy system can help take some of the pressure off your existing electric bill. Basic survival skills that include learning skills such as how to start a fire, build a shelter, and find food and water can be applied to any situation. So you don't believe the financial system will collapse. You don't have to, but you can't help but believe that there are certainly some real possibilities of other events happening that could put you in a survival situation.

- Sewing will be a skill you need to learn. You will have to repair your own clothing and possibly make your own. You need to learn how to sew with a needle and thread. Unless you have access to an old-fashioned sewing machine that is operated with a foot pedal, it is going to be all by hand. Leather working is another skill that will be valuable. Very few people in this generation have ever learned the skill. Leather working will be a valuable bartering tool.

- Gardening will be absolutely crucial to survival. Growing food isn't quite as easy putting a few seeds in the ground and waiting for food to pop up. There is some skill and training involved and you will need to know how to plant, cultivate, use trellises, manage pests, and so on.

- Cooking from scratch is going to be necessary. Ready-made foods are not going to be an option. You are going to have to learn how to prepare meals from scratch, like making bread or throwing together a hearty stew.

- Basic maintenance chores around your home are going to be on your shoulders. You need to know how to prepare your home for the winter. Knowing basic maintenance can also help you if you have to leave your home and build a shelter.

- Hunting and foraging are going to be one of your main food sources. Hunting can be rather unappealing for some, but it is a necessary task. Foraging for fruits, nuts, berries, and edible plants will help round out your diet while providing necessary nutrition. Learn how to use a bow and arrow for your hunting needs. Learn how to make snares and animal traps. When the ammo runs out, you still need a way to procure food. Learning the ins and out of fishing is also helpful.

- Basic first aid training is an absolute necessity. Take a course today and learn how to do wound care. Learn CPR and other basic skills that will help keep you and your loved ones alive. It is best to buy a book to store with your emergency supplies. It is difficult to remember everything if you are not using it on a regular basis. This is also a good idea in case you are the one who is injured and needs help.

- Natural medicine will be your only alternative. Buy a couple of books and learn how to use homeopathic remedies, herbs, and plants to heal your ailments. Eventually, Western medicine will not be available or will only available to those who have the ability to barter. Do your best to stock up on as many natural medicines as possible. These do not require a prescription and will store for long periods of time. They are significantly cheaper than prescription medicines.

Strengthening Your Position

When the economy finally collapses, it will be something that gives you plenty of warning signs. It isn't going to happen overnight. It isn't like a natural disaster that sweeps in and takes people by surprise. When you see the signs that the country is headed for financial collapse, you need to take action and start preparing your home. Unless you have a second location you plan on bugging out to, your home is going to be your fortress. You need to reinforce the windows and doors as best as possible. Keep sheets of plywood at the ready to nail over the windows. This will do two things; it will keep looters from breaking in and taking what you have and it will give the impression your home is boarded up and empty.

You will want to move as many of your valuables and tools out of view. If you have a basement, this is a good place to start storing gear. It is a good idea to have some way to defend you and your family. Whether you choose to keep a couple of knives or guns on hand, you need to be prepared to deal with those who want to take what you have. Not everybody will heed the signs and prep for a financial collapse. Those people are going to be desperate and will become violent in an attempt to get what they need to survive.

Some preppers are willing to make their home a true fortress and set up trip wires around the perimeter to warn when somebody crosses the line. This can be done with thin wire (available on-line or at army surplus stores) and some tin cans. An early warning will give you time to stop somebody from getting close to your home and putting your family at risk.

Sadly, despite your best efforts, your home may fall to unscrupulous bandits. While you are holed up in the immediate aftermath of the financial crisis, you will need to look for an alternative location. There is a chance one nation could survive the economic crunch. That nation could end up owning your property and they will be unwilling to work with those who can't pay.

Banding together with your neighbours can help you put off the overtaking in the event there is civil unrest that threatens to oust you from your home. There is most definitely strength in numbers. Talk with your neighbours about preparing for any event that would leave you on your own. Ideally, you would want to stay in your home for as long as possible. To do that, you will need help.

What You Need to Stockpile

You must assume the economy will not rebound any time

soon. It will take years before a new form of money is built up and commerce is restored. You are on your own for quite a while. You need to start stocking piling goods that will get you through the period of adjustment from buying everything you need to making everything you need.

This is a list of what you should start stockpiling today, to prepare for that day when paper money becomes worthless. Along with basic tools that you should have at the ready, you will need to stockpile some goods to help you make it through the transitional period of learning a new way to buy things.

- Canned food-variety of meats, vegetables, fruits, soups, chilli, etc...
- Freeze-dried foods
- Dried beans
- Rice
- Wheat, flour, grains
- Jerky
- Sugar
- Honey
- Dehydrated foods, variety of fruits, and veggies
- Spices-variety, don't forget salt and pepper
- Personal hygiene items; toilet paper, feminine hygiene, soap, toothpaste, razors, lotion
- Ammunition—if you choose to keep a gun
- Heirloom seeds for your garden
- Water
- Water purification methods—bleach, tablets, a way to boil the water
- Coffee/tea
- Baking supplies; baking soda, baking powder, yeast,

cooking oil
- Bug spray—for trips into the woods to get water, hunting, foraging
- First aid supplies; bandages in varying sizes, gauze, non-stick sterile pads, ACE bandage, medical tape, antihistamine, pain reliever, anti-diarrhea, antibiotic ointment, gloves
- Fish antibiotics—can be used in place of prescription meds
- Heavy-duty trash bags
- Fire starting materials-matches, lighter, flint steel
- Batteries
- Firewood

These are some of the most important items. Plan on staying in your home where you will have access to clothing and bedding and appropriate winter gear. If you are planning on bugging out, make sure you have plenty of plenty of supplies in your new location. It will be next to impossible to transport everything from your home to a new location, especially considering gas will be in short supply. Have a bug out bag on hand to get you from your home to your secondary location.

A few other things that can help make your life a little more comfortable are as follows.

- Stock up on books. Reading is a pastime that has lost popularity over the years in favour of playing video games or watching movies. Losing yourself in a story is one way to let go of the stresses of a world suffering the effects of a major financial collapse.

- Board games are another excellent way to pass the

time. Kids who have never seen a Monopoly board game will be thrilled. You can help them transition from their hi-tech toys to the entertainment of yesteryear. Don't forget to add in some puzzles and a few decks of cards.

- Tools in good condition are a must. Don't bother with cheap tools that will break in a short period of time. You will be doing a lot of work with your hands. Chopping wood with a dull axe is brutal. Have a sharpener on hand and a spare axe handle. Shovels, rakes, and other gardening tools will aid in your ability to grow food.

Chapter 4

Cashless Economics 101

There will always be a way to do business. There always has been and there always will be. Whether paper money will rear its ugly ahead again or an entirely new monetary system will be put into place is anybody's guess. There will be something that comes down the pipeline. Since the beginning of time, gold and silver have all been valuable. They will always hold value and will likely be what we revert to. You have probably heard about preppers stocking up on gold and silver coins in preparation for a financial collapse. This is because they know buying stocks and bonds, and hiding cash in the coffee can at home, will be a giant waste of time and money-money that could be used today to buy the things that will actually hold value in a post-financial collapse world.

How To Barter

While the world gains its bearings after money fails, things you need will have to be purchased via bartering. Remember back in the old days where you could trade a few head of cattle for a piece of land or something of value? Prepare to be headed back to the days of bartering for what you need.

Bartering means you trade something you have for something you want or need. Unlike the money system, there is no set price. There is a negotiation process and some things are going to be worth far more than they were in a world with paper money. Toilet paper, for example, will hold value. You have to work with your neighbour or whoever holds the toilet paper to figure out what they want that you have. Maybe they want one of your cans of freeze-dried food or a pack of batteries. Every bartering deal will be different based on the need at the time. Things that are in ample supply will hold less value. During the peak of the summer when gardens are producing, tomatoes and cucumbers are not going to be worth much in a world where everybody is growing a garden. Garden produce will be reduced to the equivalent of pennies in most trading circles.

Bartering may also be used by offering a service. If you can sew, you can offer to sew a shirt in exchange for a pack of batteries or a couple cans of stew. This is why it is important for you to learn some of those skills we talked about earlier. You may not have a lot of tangible goods you can part with, but if you have a service to offer, that will be your new job. Your payment will not be a pay-check at the end of the week. It will be in goods you need to survive.

Bartering is also a skill. You have to be prepared to offer what you think is fair, without over bidding so to speak. Evaluate supply and demand before you make your first offer or accept an offer. If the can of coffee you have is the only one in a 10-mile radius, you have something of great value and will be able to trade it for something you really need. Be wary of those who will try and offer you very little. It is a bit of a game and it does take some getting used to. Practice your poker face! Do your best to strike a real bargain especially on items that will not be on the market anytime in the near future.

Things Worth Investing In

When you are preparing for an economic collapse, you want to spend your paper money on things that will have value post-collapse. As hard as it may be to dip into that nest egg, try and imagine how you will feel when the economy collapses and all that scrimping and saving was all for naught. Every penny you put aside is gone and you will have nothing to

Gold and silver has been a valuable item for trading since ancient times as it is easily transported, is rare, useful and unlike paper currency cannot be created at will

show for it. That isn't to say you should go on a spending spree and spend every penny you have. Use common sense and do some investing in things that will hold value for years to come, no matter what the state of the economy is.

The following list includes some of the things you should be spending your money on today to secure your financial future in a world with a paper money system on its last legs.

- Gold coins
- Silver coins
- Gold and silver jewellery—can be melted down
- Sterling silver—silverware that doesn't hold much value today can be tossed in a box and melted down to get silver.
- Old jewellery with precious stones—they may be tiny today, but in no paper money world, they could come in handy for bartering purposes.

- Alcohol—it can be the cheap stuff. It will be in high demand in a world where there is a lot of stress, trouble and grief.
- Chocolate—chocolate addictions are not going to disappear. People will be willing to part with their precious items for a small taste of something from the old world.
- Candy-bags of candy are incredibly cheap today, but when paper money collapses and factories no longer produce candy, it will be a valued commodity.
- Tobacco-nicotine addictions will not go away because the dollar does. While tobacco fields are not in short supply, with no transportation system, tobacco will be in high demand the first few months following an economic collapse.
- Personal hygiene items—toilet paper and soap are two items that are fairly inexpensive, but will be elevated in price following a collapse. These items can be traded for valuables.

If you have the opportunity to buy survival gear that is incredibly inexpensive, do it. It will be extremely valuable in a world where everyone is forced to survive without the benefit of commerce and luxury. Everything you have in your home on the day the economy crashes will take on a whole new value. While things like televisions, computers, and kitchen appliances will become worthless, things like food and toilet paper will become priceless.

Conclusion

A financial collapse in a single nation would have a rippling effect. If the Euro fails, the dollar will fail and vice versa. Our nations are intertwined and when one falls the rest will tumble down soon. This isn't a far-fetched notion. The signs are there. Expert economists have been predicting this doomsday scenario for years. While we may have slightly rebounded from the crash in 2008, it was all built up by lowering the value of the dollar. The economy seems to be picking up a bit, but it only takes one event to destroy the shaky legs it has been built upon.

Invest your money wisely. Do you truly need that brand new flat screen television or could you use the money to buy silver coins or add to your stockpile of food? Keep in mind, that television will be worthless in a world without electricity, cable or the internet.

You can prepare yourself for a financial collapse by spending your money on things that will hold real value. Say the financial collapse never happens. That would be great, but it is absolutely guaranteed that the price of food and other goods will continue to rise. Can you afford to pay double for a can of soup? Beginning your food storage today ensures you will be able to eat when the price of food jumps up to a point that you are forced to do without basic necessities in order to eat.

Invest in food that will store for years or decades and you will always have a safety net to fall back on. Maybe the entire economy won't cave in, but lay-offs and cutbacks are a reality. You never know when it will strike you. Do what you can to prepare for an uncertain future and you will be able to rest easy.

From The Author

Thank you for taking the time to read this book. As an author, I understand the importance of creating books which my readers will find both enjoyable and informative. If you have the time and feel generous, please don't hesitate to leave an honest review of this book.......... Henry Hill

Other Books By Henry Hill

Prepper's Survival Pantry

Do know what you'll eat in the event of a disaster?

Survival Pantry presents the essential elements that you should consider in preparing yourself and your family for the eventuality of an unforeseen disaster. There are certain things that are necessary for humans to survive.

First, we need an adequate supply of clean water. This book will enable you determine the amount of water you will need to provide for you and your family. The quantity of water you need will depend on how severe the disaster is and how long it takes to get things back to normal. It will also depend on what sources of water that are accessible to you.

Secondly, we need an adequate supply of non-perishable food adapted to the individual needs of your family members. This book will walk you through how to compile your emergency readiness supplies and what to consider first for the short term. In addition, it will show you how you can build on the short term for a longer term supply. You will learn methods of preserving food so that it is still edible and nutritious in the future when you need it.

A major crisis always takes us by surprise, but we do not have to be unprepared. This book will provide you with peace of mind now, knowing that should something happen in the future, you have done what you can to ensure the well-being and safety of the people you love.

The Prepper's Guide To Off The Grid Survival

Have you had enough of working day in day out, paying the rising cost of living and thinking of living off the grid?

Henry Hill's guide to a off the grid living provides an eye-opening and intuitive insight into the financial and social pressures of today's society while providing an all-encompassing method to alleviate such demands on your life by what he calls, "Living Off the Grid." Hill stresses the importance of being in financial peace while maintaining a productive lifestyle.

This book is a guide for everything from household alternatives to public utilities to growing your own produce and raising livestock. This starts as simple as using solar panels to reduce dependence on the power "grid" to providing detailed instructions on how to make ethanol to cook with. Off-the-grid homes are autonomous they do not rely on municipal water supply, sewer, natural gas, electrical power grid, or similar utility services. A true off-grid house is able to operate completely independently of all traditional public utility services. Hill mainly focuses on understanding behind the modern day utilities while also emphasizing on how to manage the things without them.

This vision and mission truly include how to get started in all parts of everyday life and goes on to mature with the audience reading this book. The book literally guides you on how to grow, while growing your own food! Though the goal of this book is financial freedom in the long-term, there are significant amount of start-up costs but options are provided for those that are on the tightest of budgets to begin with.

If you are looking to go "Off the Grid" yourself or are just curious in how this lifestyle is manageable, this is a must-have book to better familiarize yourself with the subject. This eye-opening experience will almost undoubtedly either make you want to follow this lifestyle or change your consumption patterns indefinitely.